MONEY AND FINANCE

for KIDS

Thelma Ribeiro

Illustrated by Carla Rodrigues

To my son. My love. My inspiration.

Marlon is a seven-year-old boy who loves to spend time with his grandpa. They usually have a lot of adventures where they both learn new things. Do you want to learn with Marlon and Grandpa? Today, the adventure started at the grocery store when Marlon saw something that made him stop for a moment.

"Grandpa, I would like to buy this car for my collection!" said Marlon.

"I am sorry, Marlon, but I don't have extra money today to spend on that. Maybe next time," replied Grandpa.

"Money, money, money... Why do we need money for almost everything? Can you help me to get some?" queried Marlon, leaving the grocery store.

"Marlon, it is great that you are interested in money! I have some ideas of how we can learn about money today. To start, I will ask you some questions so you can also help me learn what you know about this subject" said Grandpa, very proud of his grandson's curiosity.

"**How do you think you can get money?**" he tested while both of them were walking back to Grandpa's house.

"Hm… I can get money from working! But Mom said I can't work now; I must go to school first. But sometimes, I get some money doing chores and selling something. Hey! I had a great idea! What if we make a copy of a $100 bill that Dad has in his wallet!" Marlon said as they went inside Grandpa's house.

Grandpa laughed. "Great! You are very creative. I like your ideas; let's make a note of all the alternatives you thought of to solve this money problem. We can try all the alternatives, but I am adding a question mark on the copying-a-dollar-bill alternative. I will explain the reason for that later. Okay?" Grandpa grabbed a notebook and a pencil to write down the options Marlon had presented to solve his problem. "Money appeared in our society after **bartering** became too complicated. Bartering is trading things without money."

Marlon listened to his grandpa and remembered something that had happened last week. Marlon had been at his house, eating the last slice of Grandpa's favorite cake, when Grandpa arrived and asked Marlon for a piece. Knowing that Marlon also loved that cake, Grandpa offered something to exchange. Grandpa offered Marlon a baseball card that Marlon wanted badly if Marlon would give him the piece of cake. And on that occasion, Grandpa said, "Let's trade!" and Marlon accepted, swapping a piece of the cake for a baseball card. That experience gave Marlon an idea!

"Trade! That's a good idea, Grandpa!" shouted Marlon, running from the living room to upstairs. Marlon went to Grandpa's guest room, where he stored some of his things at his grandparents' home, and ran back to the living room, saying, "I am ready for the swap!" He held his baseball bat.

Grandpa looked at Marlon and said, "Good, you added one more alternative. I will add trade on our plan," said Grandpa, writing in the notebook. "Let's start with that! What are you going to trade?"

"I will swap my baseball bat for the car I wanted at the grocery store," answered Marlon.

"Okay. So let's go back to the store so you can try to do your trade, and on the way we can continue our money conversation."

On the way to the store, Grandpa explained what money was and how it could be represented. "**Money** is something that we can exchange anytime and anywhere for a service or a product; it is a universal good. **Universal good** is something anyone could need anytime, so it would always be accepted as a payment. There are **different ways that money can be represented**: paper bills, coins, checks, and, most recently, digital. Digital money can be expended using credit cards, cellphones, smart watches, and other electronic devices."

The store wasn't very far, and soon they arrived. Marlon approached the cashier with his baseball bat in one hand and, stretching his other arm, he was able to reach the toy car made of steel on the shelf close to the cashier. "I want to buy this car, but I don't have money, can you trade for this baseball bat? It's almost new! I got it last month," exclaimed Marlon to the cashier.

The cashier looked at Marlon and shook his head. "Your baseball bat looks great. Unfortunately, we can only accept money."

Marlon turned around, returned the toy car to the shelf, and looked down. Grandpa could see that Marlon was feeling frustrated. So, he started talking. "Marlon, what you did was fantastic! Trade was a great option to solve your problem."

"Great but didn't work," moaned Marlon.

Grandpa put his arm around his beloved grandson and explained to Marlon that he didn't do anything wrong. "It didn't work only because nowadays bartering goods is not so common, at least in stores like that. But in the past, before money was invented, people traded to survive." Leaving the store, Grandpa touched his grandson's hair, trying to bring back his attention to the conversation, and said: "Do you still want that car? If you still want that car, we have a mission! We will try as many options as needed for you to get your own money. Then you can decide if you will buy that toy car or not. We cannot give up. I am very positive that you can make it!"

"I feel that no one should have created money. So it would be possible for me to barter this baseball bat and the car would be mine by now!" lamented Marlon, thinking that if money didn't exist, the cashier would have accepted the baseball bat as payment for the toy car.

"I understand your frustration. Instead of being sad, we will make a plan to get that car! And the creation of money solves a lot of problems. Who can guarantee that the cashier would accept the baseball bat?" Grandpa said decisively. As they walked back to Grandpa's house, the conversation continued. "Money was introduced in our lives exactly because not all bartering was able to be completed for many reasons. In the beginning of society, when humans started to specialize, trade was more intensively used. For example, one person learned how to farm milk cows. Another person learned how to farm chickens. If both agreed to trade, they exchanged goods," Grandpa explained while opening the front door for Marlon to come inside the house. "What do you think could go wrong in those trades?"

"If I were the cow owner, I would trade only milk for the chicken, or my cow for twenty chickens!" concluded Marlon while he went inside the house.

Marlon and Grandpa walked to the kitchen. "You are so smart! That's right! Occasionally the trade wasn't possible for different reasons; sometimes the products were not equivalent and people started to feel they had been treated unfairly, like in your example, if someone would ask to trade a cow for a chicken. In most situations that would be an unfair trade because from the cow one could have milk and more meat when compared to a chicken. Let me add one more issue," added Grandpa. "What if the chicken farmer didn't need meat or milk? Instead, the chicken farmer needed a basket?"

The boy was about to bite a cookie when he concluded, "The cow farmer would need a basket to trade for eggs! So in the past, one should trade with different people to finally get what one wanted. And maybe, could not find what one needed."

15

"Yes!" exclaimed the old man, pouring some coffee into a mug. "Can you imagine if there was an item that everyone wanted and could see value in having it all the time, so could be always traded as a universal good? When people discovered metals such as gold, silver, and bronze, people realized that metals could be used as universal goods because they were difficult to find, which makes them valuable. They are not perishable, they are able to be molded, and they can be divided," finished Grandpa.

"I got it! Trade would be much easier! And why don't we use gold as a universal good nowadays? I still don't get it. Why are we talking about gold? What I need is money," confessed Marlon, finishing his cookie.

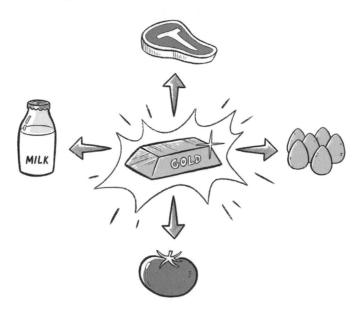

"We are close to the point, hold on! I will grab some milk for you while we finish this conversation," Grandpa said while he opened the fridge. "Gold and money are very related. The problem of using gold as a universal good to exchange created the need of the paper money."

Marlon was listening to Grandpa very carefully and remembered a movie he'd watched with his father. It was a cowboy movie where people bit the coins before accepting them as money. When he watched the film, he was surprised the coins were made of real gold. And Marlon also thought how gross it would be putting money in your month. He couldn't resist the curiosity of confirming if the movie was telling the truth, and he tested, "Grandpa, is it true that in the past, people would bite coins like I bit the cookies to make sure the coins were made of real gold?"

"Yes, some actions were needed to check the veracity of the metal, and biting was one of them. The metals also needed to be weighed to confirm how much gold the buyer had to acquire something. Two regions that today are Turkey came up with the idea of standardized sizes of metals that **originated coins**. Coins solved the weight issue. But it was challenging to make big purchases, because it was difficult to transport heavy amounts of precious metals. Do you have any idea of a solution for this problem?"

"Finally, **paper money**!" shouted Marlon.

"Marlon, that's right," continued Grandpa. "China was the first civilization that substituted the metals for pieces of paper. So you could go to the government and make a deposit of your metals, and the government would give you a piece of paper specifying the amount you have deposited; any time you needed the metal, you could go there and withdraw it. So every time one deposited or withdrew any amount, the government would give the creditor another paper with the new amount of metals that was still left. As a consequence, people started to trade the pieces of paper instead of going to the government every time they needed to obtain an item."

"I see. So it would be like a storage of gold," concluded Marlon.

"Yes, like a storage, a bank safe. However, people checked if the papers were legit. If the paper was written by the government. At a certain point, when the trust was built, people preferred the piece of paper because it was easier to carry and keep. The idea of money was created. But trust and security to make sure the paper was original from the government was a key factor. Nowadays, central banks are responsible for printing money, and they are the only institutions that are allowed to do it. The printed money has many characteristics and elements to guarantee that paper is legit. And trying to print or copy or draw money is illegal, and it's a very serious crime."

"Okay, now I understand the reason copying money is illegal and **why paper money has value**. We need gold to have money. I will cross out copying money as a solution on our notes. So I will skip the alternative of copying money, and let's go to the next alternative!" Marlon exclaimed.

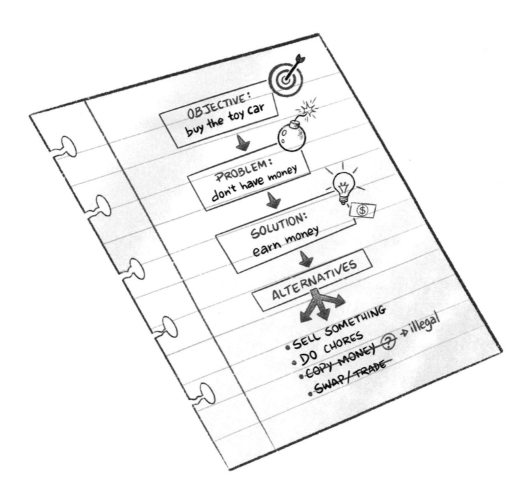

"Sure! Please cross out trading too, since I forgot to do that before. And, Marlon, securing the money with gold is how everything started. You are a really smart boy, but I will explain how the money is linked nowadays on another day, since it will take me too long to explain and we need to earn some money today," said Grandpa.

"Now, let's see what we have left! I think we still have two alternatives for earning money. You can sell something or do some chores. Do you prefer to start doing a service or selling a product? Selling a product is the same as the owner of the grocery store; the store owner buys the products and sells them for a **profit**. Profit is the difference between how much the product costs and how much the seller sold it for. In sum, you buy for less and sell for more. To make it easier to decide, why don't you write all chore options you are able to do and we can come to a price for each. And we can also plan something to sell. It's always easier to decide when we can analyze the alternatives," clarified Grandpa.

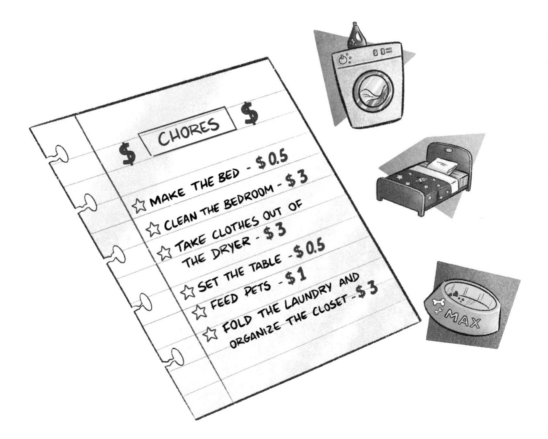

$ CHORES $

☆ MAKE THE BED - $0.5
☆ CLEAN THE BEDROOM - $3
☆ TAKE CLOTHES OUT OF THE DRYER - $3
☆ SET THE TABLE - $0.5
☆ FEED PETS - $1
☆ FOLD THE LAUNDRY AND ORGANIZE THE CLOSET - $3

Marlon thought for a while, looking at the chores lists, and decided, "I prefer to sell something. Let me think what I could sell.... Maybe I could try to sell some of my old toys?" Then, DING-DONG! The doorbell. Grandpa looked and opened the door. It was a Girl Scout selling cookies. Grandpa bought a package and said, "These cookies would go very well with a lemonade."

"I can sell lemonade and maybe tell customers some jokes," Marlon said.

"Of course you can!" confirmed Grandpa. "Before starting the lemonade, I want to listen to your joke."

"What is a bear without teeth?" asked Marlon.

Grandpa was grabbing some paper and whispered, "I don't know."

"It's a gummy bear!" shouted Marlon.

Grandpa laughed and said, "That's funny. Jokes are a great way to attract people to your lemonade stand, Marlon."

"Let me get some paper to organize your plan. You are close to achieving your mission, Marlon! You must be so proud of yourself." Grandpa positioned the paper on the table. On the paper, Grandpa wrote the cost of the lemons, sugar, and the water bottle that would be needed to prepare the lemonade. Then, he started to ask Marlon questions. "How much are you going to charge for the lemonade?"

"Buy for less and sell for more," said Marlon, repeating what Grandpa had said to him earlier.

"You are a fast learner! So to decide how much you will sell, we must add all the costs of preparing the lemonade itself," said Grandpa, writing down how much each of the ingredients to prepare the lemonade cost. After finishing the sum, Grandpa concluded, "Marlon, to prepare a jar of lemonade, we will need $2. And each jar can make 6 cups. But we will also need the cups to serve, and the package cost $1. So, how much are you going to charge for each cup of lemonade?"

- Cost of making a jar of lemonade ➡
  - $0.90 — three Lemons
  - $0.50 — 67.6 oz of water
  - $0.60 — sugar
- Cost to prepare 67.6 oz or 6 cups ➡ $2.00
- Disposable cups ➡ $1.00
- Total cost of lemonade and cups ➡ $3.00
- Cost of each cup of lemonade ➡ $0.50

Marlon read the notes on the paper and thought, $2 of ingredients plus $1 dollar of cups is equal to $3 dollars. He knew that he would need more than $3 dollars to get any profit. So he decided to charge $1.50 per cup. "The price for each cup of lemonade will be $1.50," said Marlon.

TIP FOR THE READERS:

Questions you could answer before preparing your lemonade stand:

1. How much do you suggest we can charge for each cup of lemonade? Just as a reminder, to get profit, we must charge more than it costs. Price suggestions? Marlon suggested $1.50 a cup.

2. How much will Marlon have after selling 6 cups of lemonade? Now, deducting the cost of preparing the lemonade, how much money is left?

3. How many lemonades does Marlon need to sell in order to buy the toy he wants?

4. How many lemonade cups will have to be sold in order to get the $10? Marlon decided to charge $1.50 for each cup. And he realized that selling the six cups would not be enough to get the $10. Now, is your turn to answer that question.

Marlon and Grandpa prepared the lemonade and went to the backyard to find cardboard to make the sign. They found it, and Marlon decorated while Grandpa moved a table on his front yard.

Marlon set the table with cups and a jar in front of Grandpa's house with a poster: Lemonade and Jokes. Grandpa's neighbors were curious about the jokes. In about one hour, Marlon was able to sell the six cups of lemonade. Marlon was so happy! Until Grandpa asked him, "So, do you know how much your profit is?"

Marlon drew six circles on the piece of paper and wrote $1.50 inside each of them. Then, he added $1.50 + $1.50 + $1.50 + $1.50 + $1.50 + $1.50 = $9. After, he subtracted the cost of $3. So Marlon was ready to answer: "The profit is $6 plus the $1 tip Mrs. Carson gave me for the joke. I still need $3 to buy the car!" concluded Marlon. "You should have asked that question before I set a price for the lemonade, Grandpa!" Marlon said while he was taking the empty jar to the kitchen.

"Marlon, it's your first time selling something, and you did an amazing job. The best way to learn is from our mistakes. You started the day with zero dollars. Now, you have $7! Your own money!" Grandpa exclaimed, sitting at the kitchen table.

Because Marlon still needed some money to get the toy he wanted, Grandpa asked him, "What else are you able to do that I might be interested in paying you for your service?"

Thinking of the chores options, Marlon decided, "Can I unload your dishwasher for $3?"

"Of course you can! Grandma will be very happy to learn that you did that," confirmed Grandpa.

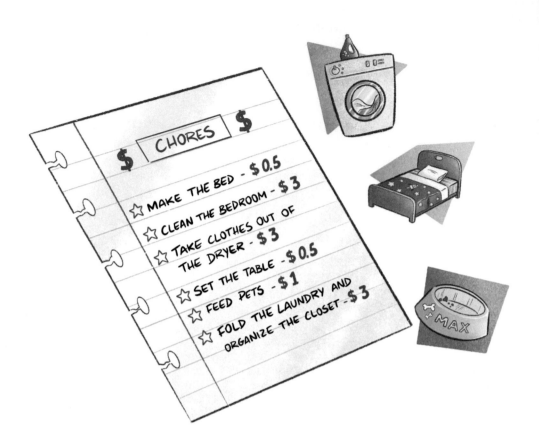

CHORES

- ☆ MAKE THE BED - $0.5
- ☆ CLEAN THE BEDROOM - $3
- ☆ TAKE CLOTHES OUT OF THE DRYER - $3
- ☆ SET THE TABLE - $0.5
- ☆ FEED PETS - $1
- ☆ FOLD THE LAUNDRY AND ORGANIZE THE CLOSET - $3

EXTRA QUESTIONS TO READERS:

• Choose two chores that Marlon could do to earn $2 .

• If Marlon wants to earn $10, which chores do you recommend he do?

• If in one month Marlon needs $25 dollars, what chores would you suggest?

By the end of the day, Marlon was tired and happy. "I can't believe it! Today I worked so hard, but I am happy that I know I can do it! I followed the plan and I earned my own money." He was able to earn the $10 that he needed to buy the toy car.

"You did it! Congratulations!" shouted Grandpa. "Now, you must think whether all the effort will be worth it to exchange your money for the toy. Let's go to the store and get that car!"

"I am not sure if I want go to the store. I will think more about the toy car later. Now, I understand when my mom says, 'This is not worth the money.' I will save the money for now," concluded Marlon, taking the notes from the table and staring at them, thinking of all he had done today.

"**Saving money** is another important lesson. Do you know why we save money?" questioned Grandpa.

"For emergencies?" supposed Marlon. That answer came very fast to his mind, since his parents were constantly mentioning that they needed to save money for rainy days.

"You are right, Marlon," Grandpa confirmed. "It is not only important to earn money, but we also need to save it! We must learn how to manage what we earned and plan for the future. We use money to spend and save. Spending is necessary to supply our necessities and enjoy our life, and pay for our **needs and wants**." Grandpa stood up.

"Marlon, do you know what the difference between need and want is?" Grandpa questioned while opening the kitchen cabinets.

"I know that! Need is when we cannot live without it, like food. And want is like my toy. I do have other toys similar to that car... but not that one, and I want it!" explained Marlon.

"You know already what need and want are. You know that we must spend our money wisely. And to save is to build a reserve to be used in the future. When for some reason we cannot earn money. So we have a reserve. We can also save money when we plan to buy something in the future. For money, we have **three different types of reserve**, and they differ by the objective for which you are saving it," Grandpa said, taking three glass pots.

"Three savings?" said Marlon in disbelief, staring at the pots Grandpa had just pulled out of the cabinet and lined on the counter.

"Yes! The first, **emergency savings or short-term savings**, is money that we need right now. For example, when your cat got sick, you needed the money immediately." Grandpa pointed to the first pot.

"The second is **mid-term savings**. After you have an emergency savings, you start to save money for a mid-term objective, something that you can wait for a little longer. To illustrate that, this savings for a kid would be the money you will need for a movie ticket that will be released in two months," continued Grandpa, moving the second pot forward.

"The third is **long-term savings**. They are named after the period of time you will need the money. And the time it will take to save enough for your objective. A long-term savings for someone like you could be a ticket for an amusement park. That would take eight months to a year if you work hard like you did today. The time when you will need the money is a very important part of the plan each of us has to build a money reserve. Today, for example, your plan was to buy the toy you wanted. However, you changed your mind and decided to save. Do you have a plan for that money you are saving?"

"I am saving the $10 maybe to buy another toy. But I will need more money," decided Marlon. "Grandpa, what are you doing with those pots?"

"Okay. Good decision, Marlon," said Grandpa, opening the drawer and getting some labels. "The pots are going to be your savings banks. How long do you think you will need to save more money to get this other toy you have in mind?"

Marlon thought and replied, "The toy I am thinking of is a board game and it is more expensive. It is $30. So I will need two or four more weeks to get it. Today was too exhausting, so I can't do that every time I come to your house. Four weeks is a lot; I think it is a mid-term savings, Grandpa."

"Marlon, you are a great saver. I also believe that for a seven-year-old, one month is a mid-term savings. And more than a year is a long-term for you. I have highlighted that the time and the savings reasons for a child like you is different compared to an adult," Grandpa said, giving the labels and the pen to Marlon.

"Why are you saying that?" asked Marlon.

"For an adult, five years is not that much; for you it is more than half of your life. For that reason, I am adjusting the time and the objectives to a child's reality. Thus for an adult's reality, short-term savings is for emergencies like when someone loses their job or needs to fix a car, so you will need the money anytime. Emergency savings are for things we cannot forecast, like a surprise. Mid-term savings is when you want to get a new car and you will need one to three years of savings until achieving the objective. You plan to achieve an objective that will take a certain period of time that is not too long. Last is the long-term savings, when you save for something like a house and you need to wait for more than five years to achieve your objective," concluded Grandpa.

Marlon was shocked. "I am glad I am a child! I can't wait that long! But thinking in long term, maybe in a year, I can get a video game!"

·EMERGENCY·
SHORT-TERM

MID-TERM

LONG-
TERM

"Marlon, you surprise me. You already have a plan! Let's grab three labels so you can stick one on each of these jars. One will be green and will represent the emergency savings. You can draw for what you are going to use the money for if you want," suggested Grandpa. "The other will be yellow for mid-term savings and the last one will be red where you save for long-term."

"Grandpa, I have a question. How do you earn your money if you don't work?" asked Marlon.

Laughing, Grandpa answered, "I am retired. I don't work anymore. Retired is when someone worked for a long time and was able to save enough money to relax and enjoy the rest of life. That's why I learned that knowing how to save money is as important as knowing how to earn money."

"Oh! You must have earned so much money to be able to save enough of it to retire," said Marlon, amazed.

"Marlon, there is another thing about money that I will say to you. There is a way we can multiply our money. The more you save it, the more you have it, and time is very important to this process. So when we create our savings, we leave our money in investments. And as long as you leave your money in investments, the more money you get in the future. Next week, we can talk about investing," ended Grandpa.

Marlon couldn't wait to learn how he could invest his money in order to multiply it. How about you?

TO BE CONTINUED...

ABOUT THE AUTHOR

Thelma Ribeiro is enthusiastic about education, cultures, and nature. She is Brazilian and moved to the USA for her Master's degree in Business Administration.

Thelma has worked in the educational industry for more than twenty years, and has wanted to be a book author since she was seven years old, but life changed this route, until she became a mother and her dream of writing books for kids grew. Her eight-year-old son is her inspiration, and she is really happy to share the content of the book in a ludic way with your kids and you.

Follow me on Instagram:
instagram.com/ribeiro.thelma

Made in the USA
Middletown, DE
12 December 2021